ABDO Publishing Company

FISH&GAME
CATFISH

Sheila Griffin Llanas

visit us at
www.abdopublishing.com

Published by ABDO Publishing Company, PO Box 398166, Minneapolis, MN 55439.
Copyright © 2014 by Abdo Consulting Group, Inc. International copyrights reserved in all
countries. No part of this book may be reproduced in any form without written permission from the
publisher. The Checkerboard Library™ is a trademark and logo of ABDO Publishing Company.

Printed in the United States of America, North Mankato, Minnesota.
112013
012014

 PRINTED ON RECYCLED PAPER

Cover Photo: Engbretson Underwater Photography
Interior Photos: Alamy pp. 5, 6–7, 14–15, 21, 23, 29; Corbis pp. 11, 13, 25; Engbretson Underwater
    Photography pp. 1, 16; Getty Images p. 9; iStockphoto pp. 12, 18, 19, 22, 27; Thinkstock p. 25

Editors: Rochelle Baltzer, Megan M. Gunderson, Bridget O'Brien
Art Direction: Neil Klinepier

Library of Congress Cataloging-in-Publication Data

Llanas, Sheila Griffin, 1958-
  Catfish / Sheila Griffin Llanas.
     pages cm. -- (Fish & game)
  Includes index.
  ISBN 978-1-62403-106-9
1. Catfishes--Juvenile literature. 2. Catfishing--Juvenile literature. I. Title.
  QL637.9.S5L53 2014
  597'.49--dc23
                        2013036760

Contents

Catfish!

There are almost 2,900 species of catfish in about 35 families. That's a lot of catfish! More than 50 species are native to North American waters. In the United States, anglers have three favorites. They are blue, flathead, and channel catfish.

Blues and flatheads can weigh more than 100 pounds (45 kg)! In 1998, a flathead caught in a Kansas reservoir weighed 123 pounds (56 kg). That giant became the flathead International Game Fish Association's all-tackle world record.

In 2010, a blue cat pulled from the Missouri River weighed in at 130 pounds (59 kg). But amazingly, in 2011, that record was topped! A 143-pound (65-kg) blue was pulled from a lake in Virginia.

The US record for a channel cat was set in 1964. The South Carolina cat weighed 58 pounds (26 kg) and measured an inch shy of four feet (1.2 m) long.

Catfish are a prized game fish. They put up a fight when hooked! A ferocious flathead seems to pull on the line like a freight train. No wonder catfish are so fun to fish!

In 2011, more than 33 million anglers dropped a line in the United States. Seven million of them were after catfish!

History

Catfish date back to the **Paleocene epoch**. They have been swimming in North America's waters for 60 million years! Dozens of species are native to North America. Most live in fresh water. But, two families include saltwater species.

For hundreds of years, people all over the world have harvested catfish for food. In North America, there is not enough wild catfish to meet this demand. Overfishing catfish populations could lead to species loss.

WILD FACTS!

Catfish are related to carp and minnows.

The long-tailed catfish is a saltwater species.

In 1963, fish farmers began to raise catfish in Arkansas. Commercial production of catfish grew rapidly. In a single year, the fish-farm industry can produce 600 million pounds (272.2 million kg) of catfish. In the United States today, Mississippi produces the most farmed catfish.

In Balance

In the United States, farm-raised catfish are **environmentally** friendly. They are raised in clean artificial ponds or inland channels and fed a vegetarian diet.

To keep wild catfish populations stable, some state natural resources departments stock waterways with catfish. This helps create a **sustainable** population of wild catfish. It also allows officials to **rehabilitate** reduced numbers of fish.

Catfish populations are not always reduced by overfishing. Hungry predators can also be a threat. In the 1960s, walking catfish were imported into the United States from Asia. This **invasive** species spread. These cats can breathe air, and they can walk across land on spiny front fins.

Walking catfish are not as great a threat to native environments. However, when they get into fish farms, they eat the growing fish. This can cause a lot of damage.

A walking catfish's pectoral fins have spikes that they use when walking.

Walking catfish were brought to Florida and sold as pets. When people emptied their fish tanks in local waterways, the mobile fish rapidly spread.

CATFISH TAXONOMY:

Kingdom: Animalia
Phylum: Chordata
Class: Actinopterygii
Order: Siluriformes

Barbels to Fins

With so many species, catfish vary in size. The micro cat can be as small as 1 to 2 inches (2.5 to 5 cm) in length! On the other end of the scale, the Mekong giant can be 10 feet (3 m) long and weigh more than 650 pounds (295 kg).

Channel, flathead, and blue cats fall between these two extremes. However, they are among the world's largest catfish.

Channel cats are blue-gray with pale bellies and dark spots. Older channels may have no spots. All channels have a notched tail. An average catch weighs one to ten pounds. A 20-pound (9-kg) channel cat is a prize catch. Anything over 30 pounds (13.5 kg) is rare.

The largest catfish species is the Mekong giant. In 2005, this one was caught in Thailand. It weighed 646 pounds (293 kg) and was nine feet long (2.7 m). It is the largest freshwater fish on record.

Flatheads, also called mud cats, are olive green to yellow brown with blotchy sides. Flathead catfish have flat heads! They also have square tails that are just slightly forked. Their lower jaws stick out.

Flatheads have a wide range of sizes. In northern **habitats**, adults could weigh 5 pounds (2.3 kg). In warm southern waters, they reach 80 pounds (36 kg) or more.

Blue catfish are monsters! Gray-blue with silvery-white bellies and forked tails, these river beasts can grow up to 100 pounds (45 kg). An average blue weighs 35 to 50 pounds (16 to 23 kg)! Giant blues have been known to snap fishing rods in half.

Catfish seem to have whiskers, as cats do. But these are not whiskers. They are barbels. Barbels are soft, not sharp. They have no sting.

Catfish have another **unique** feature. They don't have scales! Instead, catfish have skin. They do have fins, though. Some species have spines in front of their dorsal and pectoral fins. These spines are filled with **venom**. They protect the fish from predators.

WILD FACTS!

All catfish have one set of barbels on the upper jaw.
Some species have barbels on the snout and chin, too.

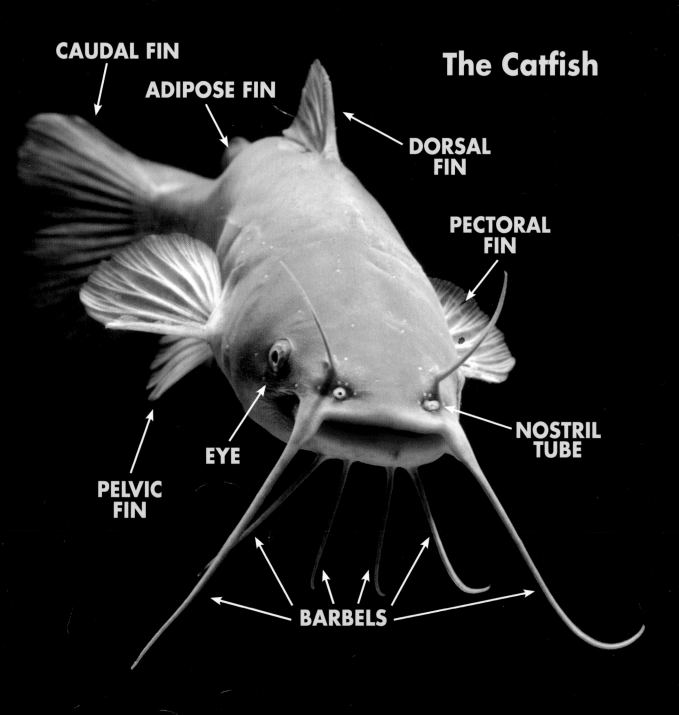

CAUDAL FIN

ADIPOSE FIN

The Catfish

DORSAL FIN

PECTORAL FIN

EYE

NOSTRIL TUBE

PELVIC FIN

BARBELS

Senses

Catfish are more active at night than during the day. However, they can easily hunt in dark, murky water. Keen senses of touch and taste help the catfish find food. When food touches a catfish's skin, the cat lunges for it!

A catfish's barbels are like an extension of its tongue. The barbels are lined with taste buds. They help catfish touch and taste food. These senses help the catfish decide if something is fit to eat.

Like other fish, catfish sense vibrations through their lateral line. This sensory organ helps fish detect temperature and water pressure changes, too. Using this information, catfish can regulate their movement and that of their prey.

The lateral line runs along a fish's sides.

Habitat

Catfish call almost any water body home. Many live in streams and rivers that have a mild to strong current. They also thrive in slow waters such as lakes, ponds, and reservoirs.

No matter where they live, catfish seek deep, private cover. They stay in their holes for much of the day. They feel secure huddled near or under boulders, log jams, dams, or sunken trees. They hide in thick weeds or deep caves called "catfish holes."

Some species, such as flatheads, are loners. They are territorial and will defend their holes. Others, like channel cats, don't mind living together.

CATFISH IN THE WORLD

Where catfish live

Even when catfish are dozing, they will bite at food that floats past their mouths. If their home waters lack a food-carrying current, cats spend more time swimming in search of food. Either way, a good catfish **habitat** offers food within easy reach!

In winter, catfish swim deep, escaping the current. Underwater, they tough out the cold. Some species grow **torpid**, and can become covered with **silt**. Others stay where they are and burrow into the mud.

Diet

Like their **habitats**, different catfish species have different eating habits, too. But, the bigger the catfish, the larger the prey! Young catfish eat algae, **zooplankton**, and insects. As they grow, cats add mussels, frogs, and small fish to their diets. Soon, they become predator carnivores.

Adult catfish will eat almost anything. They feel around their watery homes for leeches, crawfish, snails, clams, and other creatures. Some catfish even eat other catfish!

Flatheads are finicky. They prefer a diet of fresh fish. Blue and channel cats eat fruits and nuts

Ospreys are also called "fish hawks."

that drop into the water from overhanging trees. These species also eat grasshoppers and other insects from the water's surface.

In the water, many catfish are top predators. They do have enemies, however. They can be prey for larger fish. They are also not safe from eagles, ospreys, and herons.

A flathead's mouth is filled with hundreds of tiny teeth. Prey caught in that tooth pad will not wiggle or escape.

Life Cycle

Depending on where they live, catfish **spawn** from March to July. When the water warms up to around 65 to 80 degrees Fahrenheit (18° to 27°C), catfish **migrate** to smaller streams or **tributaries**. They look for warm, calm waters to make a nest.

Catfish nest in cavities. The male stakes out a hollow log or riverbank hole. He finds a spot in tangled weeds. Rocks, tree roots, or old tires make good nests too.

The male catfish lures a female to the nest. She releases sticky yellow eggs. The male fertilizes the egg mass.

In some species, the male drives the female away. The male then guards the nest. Fanning the water with his fins, he keeps **silt** from burying the eggs. In other species, both the male and female guard and fan the eggs.

WILD FACTS!

Male sea catfish carry the eggs and later the young in their mouths!

In about 10 days, the eggs hatch. The swarm of young will soon swim off on their own. Catfish reach maturity at the age of three or four years.

A male wels catfish guards his nest.

Catfishing

Laws regulate the time of year fish may be caught. They also control how many fish may be taken, and what size. Fish that are too large or small must be released. Also, check with local authorities to determine if a fishing license is required.

Before you head out, protect yourself with sunscreen and bug spray. Take along a basic first-aid kit. A flashlight, knife, and tool kit are also handy.

Anglers fish for cats from boats or piers, or by standing in shallow water. But the right tackle is key! The correct combination of rod, reel, and bait can catch more fish.

Spinning reels are also known as open-faced reels.

Fishing line is rated in pounds test. This is the amount of weight the line can lift.

TOP FIVE CATFISH BAITS

1. Shad
2. Chicken livers
3. Night crawlers
4. Crawfish
5. Homemade or store-bought dip-baits

Basic rods are made of **graphite** and **fiberglass**. They have different sensitivities and weights. There are also different types of reels to choose from. Two popular options are spinning reels and baitcasters.

A 6-foot (2-m) ultra-light rod and spinning reel with 4- to 8-pound test fishing line are good choices. Some experts advise using light tackle and lighter test line. Remember that 123-pound (56-kg) record flathead? It was caught on 12-pound test!

To bait a catfish, offer them what they like to eat. Flatheads seeking live food may bite on a swimming frog. Channel cats like dead baits. However, channels also strike at spinners, plugs, or jigs.

Bait the hook, leaving the barb exposed. To tempt catfish, lower the bait near their lair. Try not to cast a shadow on the water! You may spook the fish.

The line will go slack when it hits the bottom. A slip or Carolina rig has a sinker to keep bait floating just above the bottom. When catfish take the bait, they feel little resistance.

When the line goes **taut**, you've hooked a fish! Don't reel it in all at once. Let the catfish fight the hook. Reel in the line a bit. Then, let it out again. Repeat this until the fish grows too tired to fight.

Methods to wrestle a catch from the water to the boat depend on the fish's size. Scoop up fish with a fishnet, if the net is big enough. Pull fish up by the gills with a gaff hook or with your hands. A good pair of gloves and a fishing partner will come in handy. Don't forget to watch out for those spines!

noodling is also called handfishing.

Have You Heard of Noodling?

Noodlers reach underwater with their hands. When a catfish clamps down on the hand, the noodler pulls the fish up by the gills. Noodling looks easy. But the sport is dangerous. Noodlers must avoid other biting animals. And if they get trapped underwater they could drown. It also lowers catfish populations. In the United States, noodling is illegal in 38 states.

Got One!

When you have your catch in hand, use caution! Catfish have sharp fins, sharp teeth, and a strong bite. Their slippery skin makes them difficult to hold. To get a good grip, wear gloves or wrap the fish in a towel.

Is the fish a keeper? If the fish is too big or too small, or out of season, release it back into the water. To release a fish, remove the hook carefully. With your hands under the catfish, place it back into the water. Slowly move the fish back and forth to revive it. When the fish begins to move on its own, let go and watch it swim away.

If you caught a keeper, you will need to clean the fish. On a clean flat surface, hold the fish by its head. Snip off the sharp spines. Cut the skin behind the head and top fins. Use a pliers to peel the skin off, moving from head to tail.

Grip the fish in two hands. Crack the backbone at the head. Pull the head and guts away. Wash the meat in clean water and pat it dry. The fish is ready to cook and eat.

After you clean your fish, clean the area up, too. In the hot sun, fish guts smell badly and draw insects. Fellow anglers will thank you for safely disposing of all waste.

Channel catfish are the most eaten freshwater fish in the United States, second only to trout.

Day's End

Fishing is a tradition shared by families and friends. Fishing skills are often passed down from one person to another. The sport also brings communities of people together. Catfishing tournaments are a great way to meet other catfish anglers and gain new skills.

Fishing can be good exercise. Exercise makes the body stronger. Spending time outdoors is also a good way to manage stress.

In 2011, Americans took 369 million fishing trips! So grab a rod, head to your favorite fishing hole, and join in the fun. At the end of the day, you will have stories to tell, an adventure to remember, and maybe some catfish for dinner!

next time you go to your favorite fishing spot, you might catch a lunker!

Glossary

environment - all the surroundings that affect the growth and well-being of a living thing.

fiberglass - glass in the form of fibers used for making various products.

graphite - a soft, shiny, black form of carbon.

habitat - a place where a living thing is naturally found.

invasive - tending to spread.

migrate - to move from one place to another, often to find food.

Paleocene epoch (PAY-lee-uh-seen EH-puhk) - a period of geologic time that lasted from 66 to about 56 million years ago.

rehabilitate - to bring something back to a normal, healthy condition.

silt - fine sand or clay that is carried by water and deposited as sediment.

spawn - to produce or deposit eggs.

sustainable - relating to a method of using a resource so that the resource is not used up or damaged.